THE TRAINING TRILOGY

FACILITATION SKILLS

DICK LEATHERMAN

Published by Human Resource Development Press, Inc.
22 Amherst Road
Amherst, Massachusetts 01002
1-800-822-2801

© 1990 by International Training Consultants

Printed in the United States of America

ISBN 0-87425-143-5

All rights reserved. *It is a violation of the law* to reproduce, store in a retrieval system or transmit, in any form or by any means, electronic, mechanical, photocopying, recording or otherwise, any part of this publication without the prior written permission of HRD Press, Inc.

First printing, September, 1990

TO MY FRIENDS

Barbara Griffin, Ph.D.
Bill Griffin, Ph.D.

Shirley Foutz, Ph.D.
Bill Foutz

Carol Depp, MSW
David Depp, MSW

And of course…

Nancy P. Leatherman, M.D.

FACILITATION SKILLS

FACILITATION MODEL

FACILITATION MODEL

It's easier to understand the parts and pieces that make up effective training if we use a model — a framework — that allows us to see the whole while examining its parts. The training model we will use is the following:

☑ **1. PREPARING —**

The first step includes all of the things we do to get ready for the training program, such as sending out program notices to the participants, checking out audio/visual equipment, and setting up the training room.

☑ **2. OPENING —**

The beginning of a program is a special time that requires that a trainer do very specific things. For example, the trainer will probably need to give the group instructions about breaks, discuss the program's objectives, and determine the group's expectations.

☑ **3. ASKING —**

Good trainers take the time to find out what the participants already know about what will be taught. This information helps the trainer know what this particular group needs, as well as making it easier for the group to learn what is about to be taught.

☑ **4. ADVISING —**

This is the "presentation" portion of the teaching/learning experience, in which the trainer presents training information to the group.

☐ **5. ASSIMILATING —**

Participants need an opportunity to think about — and evaluate — new information in light of their previous experience.

☑ **6. APPLYING —**

Advising and assimilating are really mental processes for the participants. In other words, they listen while you present information, and then assimilate that new knowledge by thinking about what you said. But "thinking about," and actually "doing" (or applying), are not the same things at all. If the participants must learn a skill, they will need an opportunity to practice that skill.

☑ 7. CLOSING —

Like the opening, there are usually several things that an effective trainer will need to do in closing. For example, you may need to summarize the key things that were discussed, do some evaluation, and even present information about the next step — following up.

☑ 8. FOLLOWING UP —

We are no longer in the "training business." We are human resources development specialists! And as such, we don't just conduct training programs. We follow up to insure that if training is a solution to a specific problem, the training in fact solved the problem.

On the following pages, we will look at specific strategies and methods to use in conducting effective training programs. Using the 8-step model above, we will look at what you should do — and not do —in each of these steps.

CHAPTER 1.
PREPARING

☑ 1. PREPARING

GETTING READY

You have conducted an outstanding needs assessment, spent quality time in selecting the best training material, used additional time to modify and adapt the training material to fit your training style and your organization, and your first training session is scheduled in six weeks. Now what?

The next thing to do is to let your future participants know the who, what, when, where, and why of the upcoming training program. Confirm IN WRITING the program's time, place, and objectives. And send the bosses of the participants a copy of the same information. Then, if you or a member of your staff have the time, contacting each of the participants by phone a day or two before the session, will result in better attendance.

When you schedule the session, try to avoid Mondays and Fridays if possible. Participants may forget over the weekend that they are due at the training room on Monday at 8:30 a.m., and you will all too likely end up with stragglers and no-shows. Or, if you schedule your session for Friday, you will find that some of your participants will have—at the last minute—numerous reasons why they can't come (need to finish up the week's paper work; boss assigned a big project; need to go home early for the weekend; etc.). This can play havoc with your long-range planning when you suddenly find yourself with the need to do make-up sessions.

The following is a real letter that was sent out by a competent trainer (the names are changed).

To: Bud Allen   Linda Jazz   Ruth Nickerson
        Laura Argol   Conni Koren   Joe Tucker
        Carol Blank   Lorrie Jones   Frances Thorpe
        Lydia Williams   Kim Mullen   Sue Thurston
        Yvonne Gless   Mike Milburn

From: Bob Williams
        Training Officer

Date: 8 January

Subject: PERFORMANCE APPRAISAL PROGRAM

This memorandum is a follow-up to an earlier, verbal contact with you regarding our new Performance Appraisal Program. Your group workshop will be held on Tuesday, January 26, from 8:30 a.m. to 4:30 p.m., in the sixth floor conference room (Room 6327). As you know, we start our training sessions on time, and your presence is needed at or before 8:30. Please schedule this day so that you can stay until 4:30.

Parking will be available in our open lot adjacent to the rear of the building. Please use any space marked "Visitor," and then sign in with the security guard on the first floor.

This program will focus on the **performance appraisal interview**, NOT the system we use here at Vranso (the form, where the form goes, who signs it, and so forth). Upon completion of this workshop, you should be able to:

1. Identify supervisory behaviors that can create problems during a performance appraisal interview.
2. List the major reasons for conducting a performance appraisal.
3. Implement the detailed preparation necessary to ensure a good performance appraisal.
4. Conduct an effective appraisal interview.
5. Use a summary/follow-up procedure to ensure good communications.

As a supervisor or section leader, you hold a key position in our organization. We depend upon you to conduct quality performance appraisal interviews with your people. We are excited about this new program because we believe that it will help you to develop and enhance your leadership skills. I look forward to seeing you on the 26th. If you have any questions, please call me at 7601.

cc: Managers of the above individuals.

The day before the session begins, check out the equipment, materials, and facility. Does the video player work—and does it play the size video tape that you plan to use (1/2″ VHS, 1/2″ BETA, or 3/4″)? Does the overhead projector project properly, and is there an extra bulb? Is the overhead projector screen ready in the training room, and is it properly positioned? Is the screen positioned so that ceiling lights do not shine directly on it? Do the AC outlets work? Will you need an extension cord?

Next, do you have enough flipcharts; and do you have extra paper? Do you have magic markers for each table or sub-group—and masking tape to hang up the completed charts? Does each participant have a name tag or desk tent, a sharpened pencil, and scratch paper for note-taking?

Are your handouts ready for distribution, and do you have extra copies? Occasionally a sheet is left out of a handout, so it is wise to have an extra set or two.

The whole idea is to be professional. Your participants can't help judging the program's content by how well you are organized. So do spend time—PRIOR TO THE SESSION—making absolutely certain that everything that is needed is in place.

It's time! The training session is today—and you are its facilitator.

May I give you one piece of advice which I have learned through experience? Get up early, leave the house early, and arrive at the training room early. "Murphy's Law" will catch up with you sooner or later: what can go wrong, will go wrong! And most things that go wrong take time to fix. I have walked into a training room that I had carefully set up the night before and found tables and chair arranged completely differently. I have found projectors missing, video equipment borrowed, and the electrical power off at the outlets (we had TIME to rig an extension cord from another room).

If you're using overhead transparencies, check to make sure they have been cleaned since the last time you used them. And also make sure they are in the correct order. Double-check the overhead projector to see if it is still working! If you need to hang blank easel paper on the wall for a sub-group that doesn't have its own easel, do it now. Put out the "For your notes" scratch paper, pencils, name tags, and magic markers for each participant. The idea is to take care of all the arrangements BEFORE the participants begin arriving—when you want to be greeting each person as he or she arrives.

START THE MEETING ON TIME! Don't punish the early arrivals and reward the late-comers. If you delay the starting time, several things are going to happen—none of them desirable. First, you will develop a reputation for starting meetings late, and—guess what?—your participants will begin arriving late. Second, some participants may strongly feel that you are wasting their time by not starting on time. And third, you are going to end up in trouble meeting your time schedule.

7. Write your notes on the white frame margin of the transparency. An ordinary fine point PERMANENT transparency pen will write on white plastic frames, and an ordinary ball point pen can be used on cardboard frames.
CAUTION: DO NOT WRITE ON THE TRANSPARENCY ITSELF WITH A PERMANENT PEN! USE ONLY A TEMPORARY (ERASABLE) TRANSPARENCY PEN WHEN WRITING ON THE TRANSPARENCY FILM.

8. Read each word of a transparency as it is shown on the screen. Don't turn the overhead on and silently stand there while your group reads.

9. Make sure that you have an extra lamp bulb that fits your specific projector.

10. Don't jar the projector when the lamp is on. The lamp's filament is soft and easily broken when the projector is on, so turn it off before moving it.

11. For best participant viewing, position the overhead screen in the right hand corner of the room (as you face the participants), and place the projector in the front center of the room at an angle so that the light is centered on the screen. If you are left-handed, simply reverse the above (i.e., position the screen in the left hand corner of the front of the room).

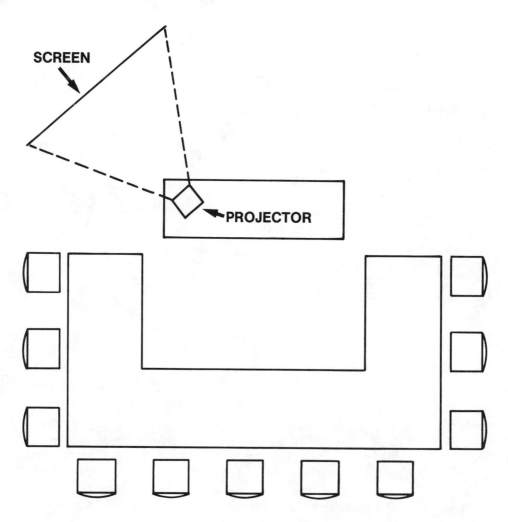

EQUIPMENT

Some parts of this section may already be familiar to you — and some won't. But even in those topic areas in which you are already competent, just remember that the "best" can become even better. Following are some tested ideas that can help you further improve your facilitation skills. And if you discover just one helpful new idea that works for you, then your investment of time has been valuable.

In this section, you will: 1) review in detail the use of the overhead transparency projector; 2) review the use of video tape; and, 3) learn some useful tips on using flip charts.

Overhead Transparencies.

Having used overhead projectors for over twenty years as a key teaching tool, I'll admit my bias. If you aren't already using this method, your trainees are being deprived of an important tool for learning.

Using Transparencies.

Transparencies are great for you, the trainer—and for the participants. They reduce your preparation time because they act as a visible outline during a program. In addition, they make it easier to maintain eye contact with the participants while presenting the program's information. And last, they increase the amount of information that can be presented in a given period of time.

But the most important reasons for using transparencies have nothing to do with us as trainers. The major reasons for using them are to: 1) improve PARTICIPANT retention of the program's ideas and concepts, 2) make it easier for them to remember training instructions, and, 3) reduce the chances of misunderstanding.

The basics of using overhead transparencies are as follows:

1. Focus and adjust the projector and screen BEFORE the class starts.

2. In almost all cases, control the group's access to the information by using the "reveal" technique, by placing a sheet of 8½" x 11" paper UNDER the transparency, and then turning the light on. Reveal each point by holding the transparency frame with one hand and pulling the paper out with the other hand, revealing one point at a time. Reveal whole thoughts or paragraphs at one time, not line by line.

3. Keep the projector light OFF unless the overhead transparency is on the projector. Turn the projector off between transparencies, as the white glare on the screen (with no transparency on the projector) can be quite distracting.

4. Leave the room light ON when using the overhead. Most overhead projectors are deliberately designed so that you can keep the room lights on as you present information. This helps you maintain eye contact with the group, and also allows them to see—and interact with—each other.

5. Do not turn around and read from the screen except on the rare occasion when you may wish to strongly emphasize a specific point. Read the information directly from the transparency as you reveal it. This allows you to maintain better eye contact with your group.

6. Use a pencil, pen or small pointer to indicate specific items on a transparency. Do not use your finger, as it looks strange when enlarged ten times on the screen!

Overhead Projector. This is not a commercial for a specific brand of overhead projector. But after using overhead projectors for many years, I have experience with many types and styles. First, my preference is always for a projector that has a switchable spare bulb. Your bulb WILL burn out—and usually at exactly the wrong time! Projector bulbs get extremely hot, and it is very difficult to replace a burned-out bulb in the middle of a program. Therefore, some brands have a lever in the back that allows you to quickly—and painlessly—replace the bulb simply by sliding a new one into the socket.

I also like a projector that has a "bar" across the front which is used as an "off" and "on" switch. This type of switch is easier to find, and also lends itself to the quick off-and-on switching techniques required when properly using overhead transparencies.

Another useful feature is a projector lens arm which folds down. This will make it easier to move the projector from location to location.

Last, the projector should have a polarized, frosted glass table top. This will keep the light spill from glaring in your eyes during an all-day program.

One type of projector I would not suggest using is the small portable. These produce excessive light glare because the design excludes a polarized glass. Portable projectors are almost guaranteed to produce a migraine headache by the end of a day-long workshop.

Thus, the overhead projection system offers these advantages:

- it allows normal room light

- it is simple to operate

- you can maintain eye contact with your group

- it saves presentation time.

An overhead projection system creates an exciting and professional presentation, and is enjoyable to use.

Video Tape. Today there is a wide variety of video formats: 8mm, 1/2″ VHS and Beta, 3/4″, 1″, and even 2″ wide video tape still seen in some older studios. How do we make sense out of this array? Fortunately, there are rules of thumb we can follow. First, 8mm, 1/2″, 3/4″, 1″, and 2″ refer to the actual width of the video tape. Second, in general, the wider the tape, the better the quality of the final television picture. Third, most trainers have little need for broadcast quality 1″ or 2″ tape. Fourth, the trend in this country has been to standardize with 1/2″ VHS tape. And last, with recent technological advances, a 1/2″ system will probably work well for most trainers today.

Video tapes also come in a variety of lengths. 30 or 60 minute 1/2″ video tapes can be purchased off the shelf, and 3/4″ tapes are available in 10, 15, 20, 30, and 60 minute lengths. Most 1/2″ video players have three speeds: SP (fastest); LP; and EP - or SLP (slowest). 3/4″ equipment usually has only one preset speed. In the case of 1/2″ tape, the slower the speed, the longer the tape will play—but the poorer the recording quality.

Because video tape equipment is so versatile (it will record and play, is relatively inexpensive, and can be used in normal room light), video has generally replaced film as the best choice for training.

If your training department has old but still usable films, it is possible to transfer the 16mm film to video. However, most of your films are likely still protected by copyright. So be sure to contact the film's producer and obtain permission BEFORE the film is copied.

PLEASE DON'T DUPLICATE COPYRIGHTED MATERIAL! I personally know of two trainers who were fired for copying. And that can be the least that happens. Today, duplicating a copyrighted tape is a federal crime punishable by fines and imprisonment. Suppliers of training materials have taken a strong and aggressive stand on unauthorized copying, and have even set up a reward program for information leading to the prosecution and conviction of anyone who duplicates copyrighted material.

Not only is copying someone else's material illegal, it is simply wrong. It just isn't fair to steal! In the long run, unauthorized copying can severely reduce a supplier's ability to recover the initial high cost of producing a video. This results in reduced investment income for the supplier, which in turn reduces the supplier's ability to create additional video tapes. In other words, why bother developing a video if users pirate it? If you need another copy or copies of a particular video tape, most suppliers have a discount structure with reduced prices for multiple copies.

Video Recording. There are two major components to consider when using video as a recording tool: video (the picture), and audio (the sound). Since video recordings are often made during practice role-playing sessions, the video camera should have a zoom lens that will allow you to position the participants so that their image fills the TV screen. But avoid unnecessary zooming in and out when actually recording. In addition, avoid "panning" the video camera left and right during a practice session. If you do need to use the zoom lens, or pan left or right during a practice role-play session, make the movement slow, and very deliberate.

If possible, avoid video cameras that have built-in microphones. If the mike is in the camera, it is going to be too far away from the "action," and will pick up unnecessary room noise. Most of the audio amplifiers that are used in video equipment have automatic gain controls which increase the amplification of the sound automatically. In other words, the farther away the participants are from the mike, the higher will be the recording volume, and the louder becomes the room's background noise. Air conditioning or heaters, chairs scraping, participants clearing their throats or coughing, all will be amplified and will tend to interfere with the audio recording of the individuals who are practicing. If possible, use a separate mike and place it near the role-play participants in order to reduce the extraneous noise.

Flip Charts. When presenting information to participants, the overhead projector is probably best. This is because the facilitator normally has time to plan what information will be presented to the participants, and also has time to create transparencies to use in communicating these ideas. Presenting concepts and ideas using an overhead transparency is usually much quicker than writing out the information on flip charts during the presentation.

But when we are receiving information from our participants, a flip chart is probably the training tool of choice for most facilitators. The major reason for using flip charts is that we can hang flip chart pages on the wall so the participants' responses are visible throughout the workshop. Thus, if we open a day-long workshop with a list of our group's "Expectations" and "Reservations," we can then tape the completed lists on the wall and refer to them throughout the day.

When using flip charts, here are several ideas that can help make you even more effective as a trainer.

1. Use only dark marker colors when writing on the easel paper. Black, dark brown, or dark blue are the most legible. Avoid using lighter colors like yellow, orange or green. Surprisingly, red is also a very difficult color to read, and should be avoided.

2. Print—don't use script. Block printing on the easel paper is much easier to read from the back of the room.

3. If possible, obtain easel paper with light, preprinted "grid" lines. This will help make your printing more legible, and will look more professional.

4. Use low-tack masking tape when taping easel paper to walls, since some types of adhesive tape will pull paint right off the wall when removed.

5. If your budget allows, obtain enough easel stands and paper so that each sub-group in a workshop can have its own easel. You should also order an extra easel to place in the front of the room for your use during the training session.

There are a great many types and styles of easels available for holding flip chart pads. Unfortunately, most are too flimsy, or heavy, to be useful. (After working with—and working on—easel stands for many years, the best one I've found is the Oravisual #A502, now made by the Da-Lite Screen Company. It is sturdy, has a back plate to support the easel pad, and folds up for storage.)

TRAINING ROOM LAYOUT

There are numerous ways of laying out a training room. But there are two primary room layouts that deserve special attention because competent trainers have discovered that they are particularly effective. First, the layout shown on page 16 illustrates the use of a "V," which gives all participants a clear and unobstructed view of the facilitator and the overhead projector screen. Another version of this type of layout is to use another table across the end to form a "U." However, the "V" is usually preferred because it gives the participants a better view of each other and of the front of the training room. The major problem with both the "V" and "U" arrangements is that additional space is usually required for break-out tables to use for small group work.

Another effective room layout is shown on page 17. The placement of separate groups at each table facilitates the transition from large group work to small group sessions. That is, the participants don't have to move for subgroup work since they are already at their individual workshop tables. If the content of a training program requires considerable small group work, then this layout should probably be selected over the "V" or the "U" arrangements.

ROOM LAYOUT #1

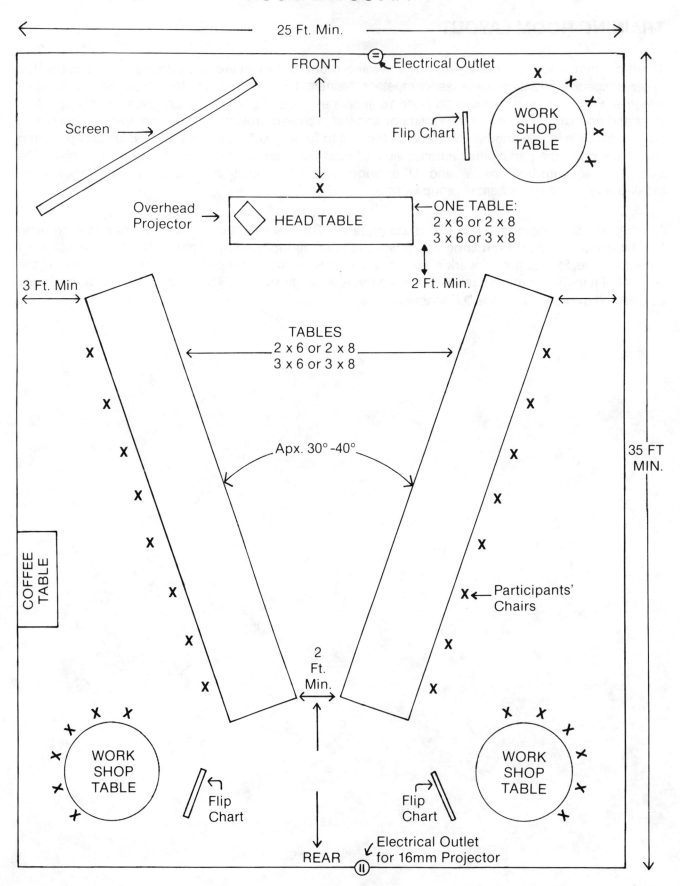

ROOM LAYOUT #2

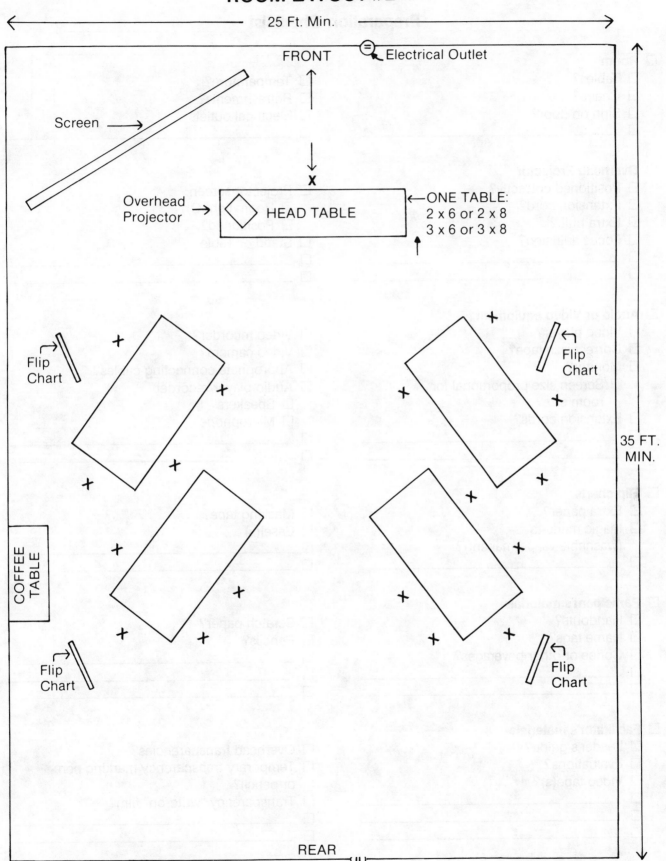

25 Ft. Min.

FRONT

Electrical Outlet

Screen

Overhead
Projector

HEAD TABLE

X

ONE TABLE:
2 x 6 or 2 x 8
3 x 6 or 3 x 8

Flip
Chart

Flip
Chart

COFFEE
TABLE

Flip
Chart

Flip
Chart

35 FT.
MIN.

REAR

17

Preparation Checklist

☐ **Room**
  - ☐ Tables?
  - ☐ Chairs?
  - ☐ Sign on door?
  - ☐ _____

  - ☐ Temperature?
  - ☐ Refreshments?
  - ☐ Electrical outlets
  - ☐ _____

☐ **Overhead Projector**
  - ☐ Positioned correctly?
  - ☐ Extension cord?
  - ☐ Extra bulb?
  - ☐ Focus adjusted?
  - ☐ _____
  - ☐ _____

  - ☐ Projector screen
    - ☐ Room light OK?
    - ☐ Positioned?
  - ☐ Stand or Table
  - ☐ _____
  - ☐ _____

☐ **Audio or Video equipment**
  - ☐ Video player?
  - ☐ Correct size tape?
  - ☐ Monitor?
    - ☐ Screen size proportional for room size?
  - ☐ Extension cords?
  - ☐ _____
  - ☐ _____

  - ☐ Video recorder?
  - ☐ Video camera?
  - ☐ Appropriate connecting cables?
  - ☐ Audio player/recorder
    - ☐ Speakers
    - ☐ Microphone
  - ☐ _____
  - ☐ _____

☐ **Flip charts**
  - ☐ Extra paper?
  - ☐ Magic markers (washable vs. permanent)?
  - ☐ _____

  - ☐ Masking tape?
  - ☐ Easel(s)
  - ☐ _____
  - ☐ _____

☐ **Participant's materials**
  - ☐ Handouts?
  - ☐ Name tags?
  - ☐ Coffee or other beverages?
  - ☐ _____
  - ☐ _____

  - ☐ Scratch paper?
  - ☐ Pencils?
  - ☐ _____
  - ☐ _____
  - ☐ _____

☐ **Facilitator's materials**
  - ☐ Leader's guide?
  - ☐ Evaluations?
  - ☐ Video tape(s)?
  - ☐ _____
  - ☐ _____
  - ☐ _____

  - ☐ Overhead transparencies?
  - ☐ Temporary transparency marking pen or pencil?
  - ☐ Transparency "write-on" film?
  - ☐ _____
  - ☐ _____

For your notes....

CHAPTER 2.
OPENING

☑ 2. OPENING

It's the beginning of your program. The participants are milling around, finding their places. The sound level is higher than normal, and the participants seem animated. You turn on the overhead projector to show your first transparency, and suddenly the participants become quiet. At this moment, they are probably as attentive—and anxious—as they will be during the training program.

At this point, you have several jobs, as follows:

1. **"Administrivia"** — You will likely have some administrative things to do at the beginning of the session: noting who is present and who isn't, telling the participants where the restrooms are, discussing break times, lunch arrangements, and quitting time, etc.

2. **Facilitator's personal disclosure** — The participants are going to have you as their leader for the duration of the training program. So it is only fair that they learn a little about who you are. Telling the participants about yourself not only helps to reduce their anxiety, but will also demonstrate a model of honest communication.

3. **Participant's introductions (if necessary)** — In some cases, the participants already know each other, but sometimes they don't. Thus, you may need to plan time to have them introduce each other.

4. **What do our participants want in this training program? What do they think they'll get? And what are they afraid they'll get (whether they want it or not)?** — Participants have many unanswered questions which can get in the way if not answered. That is why most effective trainers allow time to deal with such unspoken questions. By breaking the group into sub-groups, and having each sub-group determine their own expectations and reservations about the training program, you will help make conscious important questions. (You will be able to answer many of these questions— though not all at this point in the program.)

5. **Objectives** — Now is the time for you to tell the group what you are going to teach. If you have already determined their expectations and/or reservations, you can discuss those objectives which will meet their expectations—and those that will go beyond them.

CHAPTER 3.
ASKING

☑ 3. ASKING

As we shall see, the trainer can use questions for many purposes. But one of the most important reasons for using questions is to find out what the participants already know—or don't know—about the topic that is about to be taught.

Sure, you did a needs assessment, and you conducted verification interviews during the design of your program, but the chances are that you didn't talk individually with all the participants that are now in the room. And what they know or don't know, can have high impact on the quality of your training!

You need to know what the participants know for several reasons. First, they will learn better when you can relate the new information to their specific experience. And in order to determine their experiences, you need to ask good questions. Second, you may also need to adjust what you are about to teach in order that you don't bore them silly by telling them what they already know—or assume that they know more than they do and inadvertently omit key information. In addition, you will often find one participant that already knows what is about to be taught and you can use this participant as a resource person for the group. In other words, it is sometimes more effective to let a high knowledge participant share his or her experiences with the other participants than it is for you to present the information. And third, you may discover that the participants have learned, in the past, information that will interfere with what they are about to be taught. Or maybe it isn't contradictory information that is the problem—maybe the environment that surrounds one or more of the participants won't support what is to be taught. As a responsible trainer, you need to know this, and the way you find out is to ask. And you need to ask BEFORE you teach a specific topic.

THE SOCRATIC METHOD (USING QUESTIONS)

There are tested skills that can help a facilitator conduct a more effective training session. First, be a good listener. Since you know where you want the group to go (your objectives), you can be especially alert for responses that lead in that direction.

Next, become skilled in the art of using questions. If someone in the group asks a question, there are several ways you can handle it. You can—if you feel you have **all** the answers and want to impress everyone with your knowledge—simply give "the answer."

Or you may seek participation (the opposite of boredom!). If so, watch carefully for signs of agreement or disagreement from other members of the group, and ask them how they feel about the question. Then, sit back and enjoy a lively discussion. And do feel free to toss in pertinent facts to guide the discussion.

Why Use Questions? Questions can be used to achieve many different things.

1. Gain participant involvement.
   "How do you feel about…?"

2. Determine group members' thoughts, ideas, or opinions.
   "What is your opinion about…?"

3. Direct conversations.
   "Tom, what do you think?"

4. Involve non-participative members.
   "Bill (a non-participant), how do you feel about what Jim said?"

5. Recognize key contributors.
   "Sue, that's an interesting idea. Tell us more about it."

6. Manage classroom time.
   "OK, we've spent quite a bit of time on that question. How do you feel about the next point on our training outline?"

7. Obtain understanding by exploring both sides of an issue.
   "That's one way of looking at it. Let's look at the other side. What would happen if you…?"

Types of Questions. There are several types of questions we can use. For example, questions have been classified into four types, as follows:

1) **Closed questions** are used to direct or guide discussions, and are normally answered with a "Yes" or "No." For example, "Do you…?", "Have you…?", "Are you…?", "Would you…?", "Can you…?", and "Should you…?" are closed questions.

   Some questions in this category are perceived as requests for more information; but technically they are "closed" questions. Questions like, "Can you be more specific?" or "Could you give me an example?" are not normally answered with a "Yes" or "No," even though they are in fact closed questions.

2) **Open questions** are used to gain more information, and are not normally answered with a "Yes" or "No." Open questions that yield the most information usually start with "What" or "How." Other open questions, beginning with "When" or "Where," can serve as clarifiers, since they obtain more specific details, but are less useful for general probing.

   The least desirable question seems to be the personal "Why" question — as in, "Why did YOU do it that way?" The "why" combined with the "you" can produce defensive behavior, since it questions personal motives. However, a "Why did THEY do it that way?" is less challenging, since it asks a person for an opinion about others.

3) **Mirror statements** (sometimes called "paraphrasing") are used in place of open questions to gain more information. This technique comes from the counseling profession, and uses the following three-step model:

   1. Listen intently.
   2. Reflect the statement or question back to the participant in your OWN words ("You feel…", or "Your concern is…")
   3. Ask if your summary is correct. ("Did I understand you correctly?", or "Is that correct?")

   This technique forces you to listen extremely carefully, since you know that when the participant is finished speaking, you will need to repeat to him or her what was said. In addition, it clearly demonstrates to the participant that you really did hear and understand what was said.

   I have used this communication tool a great deal in my work, and am constantly surprised to discover that I didn't understand as well as I thought I had. Thus when I say, "Is that correct?" and the participant says "No!", I gain the important opportunity to find out what he or she really wished to express.

4) **Guided questions** are used to direct the discussion to either the positive or negative side of an issue. For example, if a participant says, "I like that communications model, but I'm not sure it will work with my people," you can guide the discussion to either side of the participant's statement by asking an appropriate question.

   Positive -   "What do you like about this particular communications model?"
   Negative -   "What are your major concerns about using this communications model with your people?"

29

Classification of Questions. We can also classify questions by looking at how they are used. For example, during a training program either the trainer or a participant can initiate a question. If the trainer initiates the question, it can be directed to a specific individual by using the participant's name first, and then asking the question. Or, the trainer may prefer to ask the whole group a question in order to avoid putting one individual on the spot. In discussing these two ways that a trainer can initiate a question, we'll label the first "Rifle" (a question directed from the leader to a specific individual in the group), and the second, "Shotgun" (a question directed from the leader to the whole group).

Leader Initiates	Example	Schematic
		Trainer Participants
Rifle (say the participant's name first)	"Bill, what do you think?"	● QUESTION → ○○○
Shotgun	"How do all of you feel?" "What ideas do you have?" "What do you think?" "What are your concerns?"	● QUESTION → ○○○

If a group member initiates the question, a trainer can respond in one of three ways. For example, he or she can relay the question back to the same participant that asked it (called "Relay-Direct"). Or, the trainer may wish to encourage participation with other members of the group either by relaying the question to the group as a whole ("Relay-Shotgun"), or by asking another participant in the group to answer the original question ("Relay-Rifle").

Group Initiates	Example	Schematic
		Trainer Participants
Relay-Direct	"That's a good point, Bill. Could you say more about it?"	● ← QUESTION ○○○ / RESPONSE →
Relay-Shotgun	"That's a good question, Bill. How do the rest of you feel?"	● ← QUESTION ○○○ / RESPONSE →
Relay-Rifle	"That's an interesting question, Bill. Betty, you've had some experience in this area. How do you handle that?"	● ← QUESTION ○○○ / RESPONSE →

Loaded Questions.   Suppose a participant said to you, the trainer, "Don't you think that this process will take too much time to use?" Look out! This participant did not ask a "question"; he or she actually stated an opinion in the form of a question. Questions like, "Don't you think...?", "Don't you feel...?", or "Wouldn't you agree that...?" are usually expressing strong opinions.

Participants often mask opinions as questions because they feel it is safer to express an opinion as a question rather than say, "I believe that...!" In this case, you might choose to relay the question directly back to the participant by saying, "So you feel that there are certain times when you are so overrun with problems that you won't have time to use this process. Is that correct?"

Now suppose this participant replies by saying, "No, that's not what I mean. We have other duties that we have to perform like meetings, handling paper work, and so on. We just have too many other things to do! Don't you agree?" At this point, not only have you helped the participant express his or her opinion, but you also discover that you have misunderstood the original question.

Did you notice the "Don't you agree?" question at the end of the participant's statement? Unfortunately, this participant is still looking for the "Official Answer from the Trainer." Here, you can tactfully choose not to answer this question by looking to see if someone (through nonverbal head-shaking in disagreement) does not agree with the first participant. If you find someone indicating an opposing view, use the "Relay-Rifle" technique to let him or her answer the first participant. For example, you might say, "Joan (the head-shaker), how do you feel about Bill's question?", and let her tell Bill why she believes that they must make time to use the process.

The payoff from using this technique is participation. The workshop participants get to the objective through focused dialogue — and at the same time enjoy doing it. The cost is time. It takes time to conduct a participative workshop. But the end results are worth the cost. Deeper growth and learning take place, the participants appreciate the process (who said learning can't be fun?) — and you can be a hero!

CHAPTER 4.
ADVISING

☑ 4. ADVISING

LEADERSHIP

A new trainer might ask, "You mean you expect ME to stand up in front of a group and lead a workshop?" You bet! Good trainers are not born knowing how to facilitate training—they learn how. And usually, they learn the hard way! Fortunately, you don't have to learn through making mistakes. If you; 1) understand the real training needs of the group, 2) develop or buy training materials that match your group's needs, and, 3) conduct PARTICIPATIVE sessions with your groups, then it is hard to go wrong. You can almost sit back and let the groups teach themselves.

Granted, there's a little more to it than that! But most serious training errors occur, 1) because the group didn't really need what was being taught; or, 2) the training processes were inappropriate for the particular group and/or subject being taught.

For example, I've observed a group of naturally talented writers being taught "Effective Writing Skills" by a trainer who used lecture and a blackboard as his only teaching process. No one in the group participated or did any actual writing; they just sat and listened to the lecture and tried to stay awake.

Participant-Centered Training. Participatin is a way of thinking. If you feel you have all the answers to life's problems, you're obsolete before you start (the questions are changing!). A leader with all of life's answers tends to conduct leader-centered sessions. In other words, the group is not allowed to participate and, in effect, is told to "sit down", shut up, and listen to me talk." What a bore! People don't like to be talked at, they like to be talked with.

35

But at the same time, good trainers recognize that it's not just a "participative" vs. "non-participative" issue. It is also an issue of leadership style — i.e., directive vs. non-directive. In other words, you can have participation without direction and end up with chaos. Or you can have participation while at the same time directing the group's learning toward the achievement of their objectives.

Leader-Centered Training.   There are times when you may choose to use a non-participative approach, such as lecturing. This method allows you to present much information in a short time, is "safe", since you are not challenged by the participants, and the presentation is not as interrupted by inappropriate questions or comments. In addition, it will also reduce the chances of your being sidetracked by the participants.

However, the disadvantages of a lecturing leadership style are many. For one, important learning through group involvement is greatly reduced. Also, this method demands high entertainment skills from the trainer. Further, the trainer may present incorrect ideas or opinions without having the opportunity to discover this fact through group interchange.

In some ways, new trainers are fortunate when they don't have all the answers—and know they don't. The problem lies in how this lack of experience is handled by the leader. If he or she covers up by playing a tough "I've-got-it-all-the-answers" role, then the program is in trouble. If, however, the leader encourages the group to develop its own answers, the meeting will be judged a much greater success at its conclusion.

PARTICIPANT BEHAVIORS

Positive Behaviors. In order to encourage appropriate participant behavior, we first need to know what constitutes desirable participant behavior, and then how we can encourage such behavior. For example, positive behavior can be any of the following:

POSITIVE PARTICIPANT BEHAVIOR

- Signals interest with:
    — Eye contact
    — Listening posture

- Participates
    — Responds positively to ideas of others
    — Listens without interrupting
    — Volunteers ideas
    — Gives examples that support discussion
    — Leads sub-group
    — Asks questions
    — Shares available class time with other participants
    — Takes notes where appropriate

- Demonstrates understanding of information
    — Completes role plays using information taught
    — Gives appropriate response to questions
    — During the training program, applies information to work experiences

- Helps keep group on topic

- Verbally supports concepts when they are challenged by another participant

- Is prompt
    — Arrives before class starts
    — Is in seat when breaks are over
    — Arrives back from lunch on time

- Doesn't leave before the end of the workshop

When we see or hear a positive participant behavior, we can encourage its continued use by providing positive reinforcement — both verbally and non-verbally. For example, as trainers we can do any of the following.

REINFORCEMENT TECHNIQUES FOR POSITIVE BEHAVIOR

- Nodding head affirmatively

- Voicing agreement ("Interesting point," "Excellent," etc.)

- Asking group to comment on point

- Repeating statement for group

- Asking participant to repeat statement for group

- Asking participant to lead discussion and/or demonstrate positive model

- Smiling

- Listening intently

- Giving special assignment

- Asking for more information on point

- Saying, "That's better than the example I had!"

- Saying, "I've never heard that expressed any better."

Participant Problem Behaviors. Unfortunately, things don't always go as well in our training programs as we might wish. True, the way that the program itself is structured (i.e., participative vs. non-participative), and our personal talents as instructors, make a big difference in the overall results of our training programs. But no matter how skillful we are, or how good the material is we are presenting, we can still encounter problems. These can occur as a result of the individuals we are training, and/or because of the specific content of the program itself. Let's look at some participant problem behaviors and their remedies.

Participant Problem Behaviors and Remedies

* Constantly tardy and/or absent
    — Identify reason in private
    — Stress importance of being on time (not fair to others)
    — Offer assistance
    — Always start meeting on time

* Challenges instructor's credibility
    — Redirect question to group or supportive individuals
    — Acknowledge this is a joint learning experience for the instructor and the participant (the leader does not have all the answers)
    — Confront issue in private
    — If you have had previous experience with this participant, communicate your expectations to the individual prior to the program
    — Ignore

* Challenges concept (negative comments on course content)
    — Redirect question to group or supportive individuals
    — Stress that techniques are not 100% effective in every case, but can increase the chances of success
    — If you have had previous experience with this participant, discuss your concerns with the participant prior to the program
    — Recognize the participant's feelings as appropriate, and move on to another point
    — Bring out positive points of issue and list on easel

* Undermines course (outside class)
    — Ensure that this participant is appointed as group leader in an early workshop
    — Confront in private, express your concern, describe negative results for others, and ask for cause and solution

* Dominates discussion (one or two participants do most of the talking)
    — Interrupt (tactfully) and relay discussion to others
    — Obtain eye contact with another participant, and move toward that person
    — Call a break (if appropriate)
    — Discuss the situation in private and ask for solution

* Does not participate
    Individual:
    — Involve in discussion by asking him or her question(s)
    — Give direct eye contact
    — Discuss in private
    — Appoint to be group leader
    — Relate to participant's experience
    — Give positive reinforcement for any contribution

Copyright 1988, I.T.C., INC.

Whole group:
— Take a break (if appropriate) and analyze cause (it might be the leader!)
— Ask more questions to get group involved
— Break up into smaller groups
— Give positive reinforcement to contributions
— Relay questions to other participants
— Ask for examples from participants' experiences
— Allude to new ideas or points to come to stimulate curiosity

* Belligerent attitude or response
— Ask participant for time to develop issue
— Write negative statement down and ask participant if it can be answered later
— Let group handle by asking for alternative solutions
— Don't disagree, but build on or around what has been said
— Appeal to sense of fairness

* Distracting side discussions (talks to individual next to him/her)
— Look at them
— Comment to group (don't look at them) "one-at-a-time, please"
— Ask group if all can hear speaker
— Ask talkers if they would like to share their ideas
— Walk over and stand near them
— Standing next to them, ask adjacent participant a question so that the new discussion is across the "talkers"
— Stop and wait (don't use unless other techniques are ineffective)

* Sidetracks discussion (leads group off subject)
— Take a break (if appropriate)
— Direct question to group that is back on the subject
— Ask how the topic relates to topic being discussed
— Use visual aides (begin writing on easel, turn on overhead projector, etc.)

Copyright 1988, I.T.C., INC.

Content Training Problems. There are some "content" problems — problems that have to do with WHAT you are teaching — that are unique to the specific program you are teaching. However, such problems are encountered in all types of programs. What follows is a list of these problems, possible causes, and some suggested solutions.

I. **Problem** — Lack of participant acceptance of program content.

    Cause — Past courses not valued by participant(s). ("This is just another theory course!")

    Solutions:

    1. Leader explains that this particular program is a practical approach vs. a theoretical one, and is based on real needs. Give examples of job-related issues this program addresses.

    2. Leader provides details of how course developed.

        a. Program was based on expressed need of this organization.

        b. Content based on actual situations that came from interviews.

II. **Problem** — Participants dislike role playing pre-written cases.

    Cause — Content of pre-written cases is not perceived as "real world" situations.

    Solutions:

    1. Participants write and then role play their own cases first. Use pre-planned cases as back-up, if necessary.

    2. Have participants prepare their individual cases before class to save time.

    3. Leader plays role in either a pre-planned or individual case as a positive model (how to do it), to demonstrate realistic behavior. (It's OK to make mistakes in order to learn. None of us is perfect.)

    4. Have participants role play past or present problems as follows:

        a. Participant "A" moves chair to face total group and describes a past or present problem related to model that is being taught. The problem selected for role play should deal with a situation where the participant (Person A) communicated with someone else (Person B).

        b. Group makes notes based on the above description, and questions Participant "A" to get all information required.

        c. Participant "A" plays role of his or her employee. One of the other participants plays the role of the other person (B), using the key behaviors that have been taught.

Copyright 1988, I.T.C., INC.

5. Another version of the above is to have each of the group members take the role of Person "B" interacting with Person "A." Each participant role plays only one of the key steps, going around the group until all steps are covered. This increases participation.

III. **Problem** — Concern that after the training session the participants are not applying the skills that were taught. (I.e., How do we know if they are being used?)

A. **Cause** — Lack of formal feedback system.

Solutions:

1. Have all participants fill out a brief summary sheet for occasions when skills learned will be used.

   a. To help plan the transition from the classroom to the job.

   b. To serve as documentation for further discussion and follow-up.

2. Conduct a departmental survey using anonymous responses from participants regarding use.

3. Make sure the participants' immediate supervisor is involved in all training, and is prepared to follow-up with the participants.

B. **Cause** — Not everyone who was taught the skills will use them.
   — Seems too time consuming.
   — Seems difficult to implement.
   — Fear that it will increase the participant's responsibility.

Solutions:

1. Encourage use by participants by ensuring that their immediate supervisors are prepared to:

   a. Give positive feedback when use of specific skill is observed.

   b. Discuss use of skills that were taught when Merit Increase given (use of skills is rewarded in a tangible way).

   c. Discuss use during developmental reviews or year-end performance appraisals.

2. Be sure managers use the skills their people were taught in carrying out their responsibilities (model behavior).

3. Provide follow-up coaching with individual participants where needed or requested.

Copyright 1988, I.T.C., INC.

IV. **Problem** — Participants becoming bored with training sessions.

A. **Cause** — Repetition and/or predictable format.

Solutions:

1. Have group develop their own step-by-step model before showing them the "official" steps.

2. Use different media (i.e., if transparencies are always used, use flip charts for a change of pace).

3. Use more small group work rather than lecture.

4. Introduce the topic by using a related problem that is currently of great interest.

B. **Cause** — Leader and/or group mix (lack of new blood in group).

Solutions:

1. Bring in new people.

2. Mix participants between training groups within a department.

C. **Cause** — Group too small (limits interaction between participants).

Solutions:

1. Combine two small groups.

2. Select and combine two conflict groups.

D. **Cause** — Role plays are too highly structured.

Solutions

1. Use different role play structure.

2. Leader participates in role plays.

3. Have real life cases filled out in advance of sessions by participants.

4. Use their own cases for role play. Use prepared cases as back-up.

5. Have two participants role play a negative model to add interest at the start of the session. Participants prepare in advance.

6. Where appropriate, shorten the training session by eliminating entire segments of a module.

7. Assign new group leaders for each role play, or for sub-group work.

Copyright 1988, I.T.C., INC.

43

E. Cause — 100% of training for 20% need (i.e., some participants don't need the training as much as others).

Solutions:

1. Use the 80% less needy participants to reinforce the steps for the 20% by:

    a. Assigning one of the 80% to lead session.

    b. Making one good and one less effective participant partners for role play.

F. Cause — One participant resists learning.

Solutions:

1. Get him or her involved by assigning leadership for a module or segment of a module.

2. Counseling on an individual basis. Facilitator should:

    a. Find out why the participant is not feeling good about the program.

    b. State his or her expectations of participants.

3. Follow up to see if he or she uses skills taught on the job.

G. Cause — Leader bored.

Solutions:

1. Try something new in each session.

2. Review with another trainer.

3. Pick a leader from the group, and team teach with this individual.

4. Have trainer's boss or another manager attend session.

H. Cause — Perception that training is not realistic.

Solution:

1. Encourage participants to apply steps using their own personal style.

2. Invite management to:

    a. Sit in as observers.

    b. Participate in role play.

    c. Teach a module or segment of a module using realistic examples from work setting.

Copyright 1988, I.T.C., INC.

3. Introduce organization, department, section information, and goals relative to the specific module being taught.

I. Cause — Training not valued (past courses "didn't change anything").

Solution:

1. Use examples of results from past training.

2. Challenge group to "change things" this time around.

Copyright 1988, I.T.C., INC.

READING ASSIGNMENTS

Prior to Class. In order to save time, we may be tempted to give a reading assignment prior to the training session. Unfortunately, problems with this strategy often occur when participants forget to read the assignment, don't have time to read it, or for some reason don't receive the assignment.

When this happens with a critical reading assignment, it makes it difficult to get all the participants to the same knowledge level during the training session. Of course, you can send out the assignment and then follow up to make sure that the participants received it and will read it. But that will take a significant amount of time. All things considered, pre-conference reading assignments are as likely to create problems as they are to solve them.

In-Class Assignments. Because participants have drastically different reading speeds, it is probably best to limit reading assignments to one or two pages at any one time. Limiting the assignment will keep the fast readers from becoming bored while they wait for slower readers to finish.

In-class reading assignments can be used to reinforce points that have already been covered, or to gain additional knowledge on concepts previously discussed. They can also be used as a "change of pace." For example, instead of playing a video tape, you might choose to let the participants read a "script" in order to identify key learning points. In addition, in-class reading can be used to give the participants instructions for specific exercises.

HANDOUTS

I am heavily biased in favor of handouts — for a number of important reasons. The first is that I value, and use, overhead transparencies in most of the programs I have developed. And when using overheads, handouts are a must! With the use of overheads, information can be transmitted rapidly to the participants — too rapidly for the note-takers in the group. When you project the first good content transparency, many participants will frantically try to copy the key ideas — and get about half of the transparency copied by the time you are ready to project the next one. By the end of the day there are bound to be some hostile participants. Or, the other option is to wait for the note-takers to copy everything you are presenting. If you do this however, you probably won't complete your program in the allotted time.

But, if the participants don't have to worry about taking notes because you have provided them with prepared handouts, it will free them to pay attention to you and to the other participants. This will result in much greater involvement and less "busy work" for the participants.

Another major value of handouts is that the participants can refer back to them at a later time to refresh their memory on the content of the program. For example, the participants may have just been taught how to conduct a performance appraisal interview; but they may not need to use the new skills until several months after the training program. In addition, detailed information can be referenced in the handouts when there is no time to cover the complete subject in the workshop.

If you decide to use handouts in your program, tell the participants as the session begins that handouts will be provided. You would hate to take notes all day (getting increasingly annoyed about the lack of handouts), and then be "surprised" with an excellent set of handouts at the end of the program.

When you pass out handouts in the beginning of a program, ask the participants to put them away, unless instructed otherwise. And tell them why! I ask my groups not to immediately start reading the handouts, because I believe in participation. I ask many questions when presenting a training program. If the participants have their handouts open to the information that is being taught, they tend to give "textbook" answers rather than their actual ideas and experiences. And I don't want "book" answers; I want their thoughts and feelings. In addition, other participants may not have a chance to express their ideas (based on their own experiences) if another participant immediately gives the "correct" answer.

"STUDENT" TEACHING

Student teaching is a favorite training tool of some graduate school professors. The class time is divided into as many segments as there are students, and each student is assigned a specific topic to present (or what's worse, the same topic). The presentations seldom involve participation.

Part of the professor's idea is, of course, to provide feedback on the knowledge gained by the students. All too often, though, this is a nice way for the professor to take some of the load off his or her teaching schedule. What is even more upsetting, is that this teaching strategy is encountered in some adult education programs on how to teach adults. The danger is that graduates — who later become trainers — may see this method of training as a positive model of how to train employees in the work place.

As you can see, I don't favor this method of teaching. It is often another example of the "sit back, shut up and listen to my lecture" strategy — except that in this version, the participants get to bore each other. I do agree that a valuable way of learning something is to have to teach it. But having sat through literally hundreds of such presentations, I am unconvinced that this is really quality training or learning.

If you do decide to use some student teaching in your workshop or seminar, the participants are probably going to need help with their presentations. Your job will be to suggest resources for content, provide one-on-one review and coaching before the participants' presentations, and help participants create innovative and effective ways to "teach" the information.

TEAM TEACHING

Pro and Con. There are real benefits from team training. First, it is nice to have back-up support when things aren't going well. For instance, we've all had "problem" participants who were argumentative —or just plain obnoxious. Difficult participants seem much easier to handle when two trainers are supporting each other.

Team trainers can also utilize each other's strengths to make the program even better for the participants. For example, one trainer might be highly skilled at non-directive facilitation and thus be a better leader for group discussion. The other trainer might be a great "edu-tainer," and better able to raise the group's interest level right after lunch. Or the trainers might be knowledgeable about different parts of the subject being taught.

If your group is heterogeneous, team trainers might match the needs of the group better. For example, a workshop on "Sexual Harassment" with a mixed group of males and females might best be taught using a male and female training team. Or a cross-cultural, team-building workshop might be better taught by an individual from each culture.

It is also nice to have help in facilitating sub-group work. When the participants are role playing at separate tables, two trainers can provide better coverage than only one.

Two trainers can act as each other's time-keepers, and help keep one another "on track." They can also help each other with mechanical tasks, like one writing out the group's comments on an easel while the other is facilitating the discussion.

The above advantages of team teaching deal with making the session more effective for the trainees. But another reason has to do with you, the trainer. How do you get appropriate and effective feedback on your own training skills if you always teach alone? The majority of our participants are not skilled trainers. So although they may know good training when they experience it, they may not know enough about the processes we use in training to be able to provide us with accurate feedback.

Another reason for team teaching is that it allows the trainer to rest and regroup at intervals throughout the session. It is generally less fatiguing to have help in leading a group. As you know, teaching a group of alert adults for eight hours can be terribly exhausting. It is nice to be able to stand back and let your partner take over while you catch your breath and evaluate your efforts.

But it is only less tiring if you and your partner take turns leading the session (sequential training). If the two of you team teach by being co-leaders, it can be just as tiring as facilitating by yourself. Of course, participants can benefit by co-teaching since the two trainers up front can together increase the effectiveness of a program.

There are some disadvantages to the team teaching approach. Two or more trainers are expensive! Therefore, the additional training cost of a second trainer must be offset by the program's importance. Also, the training styles and/or needs of the trainers may be incompatible. For example, my need is to always arrive early and have the training room organized before the trainees arrive. If my partner needs to sleep late and sees no problem in arriving at the last minute, then we have a problem.

Doing It. Team trainers Dianne and Dennis LaMountain stress the need for detailed preparation. They feel that preparation is even more important when team training because of issues unique to this method of training. For example, the two individuals involved need to thoroughly discuss, review, and practice the content. In addition, they need to know who is going to cover exactly what material, discuss the hand signals they will use, figure out how they will manage transitions, and decide when they will meet for mid-course critique and corrections. They may also need to rehearse demonstrations, decide how specific behaviors will be modeled, and determine ahead of time who will take the lead. To discuss such details properly will take about twice as much preparation time as is needed for single-trainer preparation.

At a recent national training convention, one of the participants in a Team Training workshop brought up the matter of intimacy between team trainers. He said that in a training workshop he attended, the two trainers had such a good thing going between them that the participants wondered why they were needed! He pointed out that the trainers talked more to each other than they did with participants, saying things like, "Thanks for sharing that with me, Bill. Could I now give you some feedback on how really upset that makes me?" Thus they spent more time processing what they said to each other in front of the group than with the participants.

Other problems can occur when training with a partner, such as cutting into each other's time, interrupting one another, and the more experienced trainer taking control of the session. Experienced trainers need to guard against being the "star," and showing up a less experienced partner. The less experienced trainer needs to know that his or her partner can be a safety net in case of trouble — but at the same time, not expect constantly to be "rescued." Trainers should discuss these issues explicitly prior to the session.

When team teaching, you don't need continuous mini-introductions. For example, as you transition from one trainer to the other, you don't need to say, "And now here is Dick who will talk with you about..."; or "OK, Joan, I'll turn it over to you," to which Joan responds by saying, "Thanks, Tom. OK, gang, let's talk about..." Many transitions from one trainer to the other can be handled non-verbally by one trainer simply standing when he or she has something to say, or is ready to take over.

Team teaching is not for everyone, and not for every group. But where it is appropriate, it can lead to remarkably positive experiences for your group — and for you.

CHAPTER 5.
ASSIMILATING

☑ 5. ASSIMILATING

BEHAVIORAL MODELING (be•hav′•ior•al mod′•el•ing) *n.* : A process of learning in which appropriate behaviors are taught by, 1) discussing the key behaviors, 2) demonstrating those same behaviors, and, 3) practicing to develop skills in using the behaviors.

— R. Leatherman

Historical Perspective. Behavioral modeling, as a training took, is well-suited for teaching interactive job skills. For example, behavioral modeling could be used to teach "Face-to-Face Communications" to supervisors or customer service employees, "Selling Skills" to salespersons, or "Technical Skills," like welding or data process entry, to employees. Behavioral modeling has been used extensively in recent years to teach basic skills like "Delegation," "Coaching and Counseling," "Performance Appraisal Interviewing," and a host of other topics.

In order to make behavioral modeling a viable teaching and learning process for organizations today, the following three things were needed:

1. A strategy of learning and teaching based on modeling behavior.

2. Specific content to be taught.

3. Low-cost modeling media.

Behavioral modeling, as a training strategy, has been around a long time. Apprenticeship programs, guilds, and craft training programs are all examples of job skills long taught by modeling. But it wasn't until 1917 that the earliest recorded behavioral modeling training for leaders occurred. America had just entered the war, and ships were desperately needed to transport war goods to the Allies in Europe. There were sixty-one shipyards with 50,000 new workers that had to be trained immediately.

Charles R. Allen was chosen as the head of the education and training section of the U.S. Emergency Fleet Corporation. Allen and his assistant, Mike Kane, instituted a four-step training process that was taught to the supervisors of the shipyard employees. This process — "Tell, Show, Do and Check" —was printed in card form in 1920 and used at the Dunwoody Institute by Charles Allen.

Prior to this time, the major emphasis was on the production of goods and services through better equipment and more efficient workers. In Fredric Taylor's *The Principles of Scientific Management*, written in 1911, there is not one mention of leadership training. In fact, it wasn't until 1914, in Frank Gilbreth's *Primer of Scientific Management*, that leadership training was briefly mentioned when he wrote, "...the teachers of our trade schools will soon be able to turn out teachers of mechanics, that is, foremen." It is interesting to note that the first leadership training was to teach leaders how to train, and the training process they were taught was what we now call "behavioral modeling" ("Tell, Show, Do, Check").

The use of modeling in teaching behaviors is not just a common sense approach to training. It has been well researched and documented by several noted behavioral scientists. Albert Bandura discussed the use of "higher-order vicarious learning" by employing a "model" who not only modeled specific behaviors, but also received a positive reward. In addition, he developed the notion of "observational learning" as a result of two systems, "imaginal" and "verbal."

Imaginal (from the word "image") learning is the learning that naturally takes place when we observe a behavior in another. Verbal learning is an additional aid to imaginal learning, wherein verbal cues are given as the behavior is enacted. Finally, Bandura also described the need to have the viewer's observing behavior enhanced and focused through arrangements of appropriate incentive conditions, and retention of behaviors learned by role playing.

Goldstein and Sorcher, two researchers at the General Electric Company, described in great detail specific model characteristics (sex, race, status, etc.), modeling display characteristics (the way the model looks to the viewer, difficulty of the behaviors that are modeled, frequency of the behaviors, etc.), and observer characteristics (instructions to model, similarity to the model, attraction of the model, reward for engaging the modeled behavior, etc.). Most of Goldstein and Sorcher's ideas for modeling as a learning tool seem to be gleaned directly from Bandura's earlier work.

Goldstein and Sorcher also wrote extensively on the use of role play, and established behavior change as a positive function of the following:

1. Perception of participant choice whether or not to role play.
2. Commitment to the behavior being practiced.
3. Degree of improvisation allowed.
4. Reinforcement for role playing behaviors.

Last, Goldstein and Sorcher discussed the mechanisms and principles for transfer of behaviors learned to the participant's job. The essential principles are:

1. Provide trainee with realistic key behaviors that can be later used on the job.
2. Use realistic models to show the key behaviors that were taught.
3. Provide high levels of practice and "overlearning" of the key behaviors.
4. Set up on-the-job performance feedback.

Behavioral Modeling as a Training Tool. There are three major ways to use behavioral modeling as a training tool: 1) you the trainer model the appropriate behaviors; 2) the participants are asked to model the behaviors; and, 3) a prerecorded video tape is used as a model. Each of these strategies for modeling appropriate (or inappropriate) behaviors has its advantages and disadvantages.

The Trainer as a Model. Several important advantages exist when the facilitator/trainer acts as a role model for a set of specific behaviors. First, it is much easier for a trainer to demonstrate a set of behaviors than it is to make a video tape. Secondly, the credibility of the trainer (and even the workshop) is enhanced if he or she can model the behaviors that are being taught. In addition, the trainer can model specific behaviors at different times throughout the program, whereas a video tape model is normally used only one time. Finally, the trainer as model is less expensive than a video tape.

In general, if you choose to be your own model, model only single sets of behaviors. It is a lot easier to model only one behavior than to try to model, say, the "nine key steps in delegation." Thus, simple communications behaviors, like "paraphrasing," using "open" questions, or using one step in "conducting effective performance appraisals," are usually easier to model than more complex behaviors.

Using Participants as Models. Using a participant as a model is fraught with potential danger. Before using an individual in your group to model a behavior, that person MUST be completely familiar with the behavior, and be comfortable in acting out the behavior in front of his or her peers.

So if you decide to let a participant model a behavior, ask for a volunteer, and suggest that whoever volunteers needs to be comfortable with the behavior. You can also provide a "script" or other memory aid to assist the participant as the behavior is modeled. You may even choose to select an especially qualified "volunteer," and provide some additional coaching prior to the time that the participant will model the behavior. It is also wise to limit the participant's demonstration to only one behavior, avoiding more complex sets of behaviors. In addition, the participants can be "let off the hook" by telling them that "whatever is modeled is not expected to be perfect." When the above suggestions are followed, the chances are much better that the participant will be able to actually model the behavior in a positive way.

On the other hand, asking a participant to model specific behaviors does have some advantages. It can demonstrate to the other participants that they too can use the behaviors, and will thus increase the group's acceptance. In addition, it can give you, the facilitator, additional feedback on the participants' ability to actually use the behaviors being taught. It will also raise the interest level of the group by placing their own peers in the "hot seat." And last, the participant who volunteers for the demonstration will gain additional practice time and increase his or her ability to use the new skill back on the job.

Using Video Models. Prerecorded video tape models can be expensive — especially if you try to make your own. However, reasonably priced modeling tapes that cover many different topics are available today from a variety of training producers.

Most commercially available modeling tapes are very generic in nature and may not fit your specific environment. On the other hand, the more accurately the model portrays your participant's job environment, the more the participants tend to focus on the content of the video (the actors and how well the "real" job is portrayed) rather than on the process learning points. So it is a trade off. You want the participants to be able to relate to the video (i.e., the video "story" mirrors their job environment) but not to think, "We don't do it that way here!" (the video's story line is so different from their environment that they don't accept the teaching points).

Another problem with video tape models is that they can easily become outdated. Hair lengths change, clothing styles change, and even our language changes. I know of a wonderful modeling tape that refers to a now non-existent football league and team. Naturally, some participants are distracted by this reference and perceive the content as being archaic (correctly), and the teaching points as being inappropriate (even though they are just as valid today as when the tape was made).

Video tape models also tend to be a passive way of learning. In other words, the participants are not as involved as they would be if they were acting as models. (Note: there are interesting ways of using video modeling tapes that can help overcome this problem—to be mentioned later.)

Video tapes do, however, have some clear advantages. They can effectively model a whole series of complex behaviors, and can be replayed as many times as needed to ensure that the participants have learned the key behaviors that are modeled. In addition, video tapes can be loaned out to individual employees for self-study. Good actors and production techniques can result in video models that are believable, and therefore encourage the participants to use the behaviors that are taught.

Video tapes can be used in a variety of interesting ways. For example, it is sometimes just as important to know what NOT to do as what to do. Therefore, negative models can be used to model inappropriate behavior — that is, how NOT to do something. Negative models are also fun for the participants to view. Simply show the negative model, after asking your group to "see how many things you can identify that the person in the video does ineffectively." They will discover things done "wrong" that even the writer or producer didn't notice!

You can also use a video modeling tape which does NOT have sub-titles that identify the key behaviors, and show this tape before teaching the key behaviors. Then, ask your group to identify the major behaviors that were used in the video. Next, reinforce their work by presenting the "official" key behaviors, pointing out the similarities and differences between their ideas or "labels" and the key behaviors/labels you have identified. Their observations are not "wrong," but only another way of looking at what occurred in the model.

If you prefer, you can teach the behaviors first, and then use the video tape to model them. A good strategy that will usually get your group more involved is to first teach the behaviors, then play the modeling tape, and last, ask them to identify the things that were done well, as well as the things that they would have done differently.

CHAPTER 6.
APPLYING

☑ 6. APPLYING

ROLE PLAYING "OK gang, let's role play!" Few statements will cause as much participant apprehension as this one. And for good reason. Many participants have had negative experiences with role playing facilitated by an ineffective trainer.

I once participated in a workshop where the facilitator passed out a case that had nothing to do with our jobs. He then gave us only a few minutes to prepare for the role playing session before telling two of us to sit at a table in front of the room. He next asked the group to look for all the things the two of us did WRONG — and then walked to the back of the room and turned on the video camera. My role playing partner and I not only made numerous mistakes during the role play (and got heavily criticized later), but then had the pleasure of watching the mistakes again on the video. It was NOT a positive learning experience, and left me with a bad taste for role play.

But skill practice is critically important! So the question is: how can we give our participants an opportunity to practice specific skills without making the experience traumatic? Here are some suggestions:

1. Make sure the participants have had ample opportunity to learn what they are going to role play (by discussing and then watching a model of the behaviors that will be practiced).

2. If you are using prepared cases, try as much as possible to have the situations fit the participants' actual jobs. It is hard enough to try to role play new behaviors without having to grasp new job content as well. One of the best strategies I have seen is to let the participants create their own "real" cases based on their past experiences.

3. Avoid, if possible, having participants move to the front of the room to role play. Many people become very anxious when asked to move out of their seats to perform in front of everybody else. If you have placed the participants in small groups at individual tables (3 to 5 at a table), you can almost always have them role play from their original seats.

4. Let groups role play simultaneously. Obviously you can't be at all of the tables at the same time; but you don't need to be! Let the participants themselves be responsible for observing and then providing feedback. If you want to add your feedback on the role playing, simply observe, in rotation, one role play at each of the tables.

5. If you delegate the responsibility of observing and providing feedback to the participants themselves, then briefly teach them how and what to observe before you start the practice sessions. Provide each observer with a pre-planned "check sheet" that lists the specific behaviors they will be observing. Then, tell the "observers":

   A. take brief written notes DURING the role play on what is being observed. A five-to-fifteen minute role play doesn't sound like much time, but it is a LOT of conversation. If notes are not taken, the observers will be hard pressed to come up with much more than, "That was a good job."

   B. they must be prepared to look not only for what needs to be improved, but what was done well in the role playing session.

   C. allow the individuals who were role playing to be the first to comment on the things they liked about what was done, as well as how they would improve it. Then the observers may provide their feedback.

   D. no feedback is needed on the role players' "nervousness." Participants who are practicing a new skill for the first time can expect to be nervous!

   E. they (the observers) should stay out of the practice session unless invited to intervene by the individuals who are role playing.

6. If each table is to be responsible for its own learning, you should ask each group to appoint a timekeeper to insure that all individuals have equal opportunity to role play.

7. Ask the participants in the role play not to deliberately "ham it up" for the benefit of the observers. Role play is difficult at best — and it becomes impossible when your partner is trying to be a comedian.

8. Role plays at individual tables work best when there are only four participants per table — two role players and two observers. Five participants are usually too many, and will significantly increase the role play time (around 20%); while with three participants, there is often not enough observation. In general, the feedback and discussion after a role play is much better with two observers.

9. Don't mix participants and their bosses at the same table! If possible, don't even mix them in the same room. It is not fair to ask someone to attempt to apply new knowledge and have the boss watching at the same time.

10. Timing, of course, depends on what is being role played (how complex the situation), and the number of participants at each table. But in general, with four people per table each role play will take approximately 15 minutes — 10 minutes for playing the role and 5 minutes for feedback and discussion from the two observers. The roles are rotated at each table so that each participant has a chance to be a role player, a partner for the role player, and an observer twice. Total time for one complete practice session will then take about one hour.

If you feel that you must use video cameras to record the role play, plan on spending a LOT more time! The amount of time needed depends on a number of variables. First, if you videotape at each table in rotation, only one team at each table will have an opportunity to be recorded. Second, if you MUST videotape each person in the group in front of their peers, then try to obtain a second video play-back unit. With these two units, the group can observe while a participant is recorded on video. As the group observes, they also take specific written notes on what the role player did or said. At the conclusion of the role play, the group discusses its findings (both positive comments as well as areas for improvement). Next, the video tape is played in private (by the participant who was recorded) on the second video machine (using earphones if the machine is in the same room), while the next team of two is being recorded and discussed.

If you are doing individually-recorded role plays, in front of the group as a whole, the size of the group will have a great impact on the amount of time that will be needed. If the group size is 12 to 16, it will take a least a full day to have every participant role play.

Role Reversal.
One of the best ways of learning is to use role reversal in a role play practice session. For example, if I am facilitating a workshop on coaching skills, I would first teach the key behaviors required, next show how a coaching session should be conducted, and then have the participants write up and prepare to role play real, past coaching situations. Last, I would ask one participant in the role play to be his or her own employee, and their role playing partner to be that employee's supervisor.

Constructing a practice session like this does two things. First, the participant who is playing the role of his or her employee (or client, customer, etc.) has intimate knowledge of the actual situation, and thus will be able to model the "real" employee or client. This makes the practice session more believable, and helps the participants better accept the concepts being taught. In addition, the "supervisor" (or customer contact person) in this particular role play usually does not need to know the details of the situation, as he or she is practicing the key behaviors and can generally take his or her cues from the "employee" or "client."

Second, a role reversal usually gives the participants empathy for how someone else feels. When the participants can see the situation from the other person's point of view, they often become better supervisors, managers, customer contact people or salespersons.

Using Cases.
In using cases, you have two main choices: create your own generic cases, or have the participants create them.

Generic Cases.
If you write your own cases for the participants to use in their role plays, don't let the content get in the way of the learning. In other words, if you are the trainer in a financial institution, and you use an industrial situation for the participant's role play, you are headed for trouble.

You can obtain content for your cases by interviewing future participants. Or you may have enough information from your original needs assessment interviews to write cases that are realistic. If you purchase a quality training program for the topic that you will be teaching, there might be cases included in the package. Given pre-written cases, it is usually easy to modify them to fit your specific work environment.

"Real" Cases Prepared by Participants. However, the best strategy is to let your participants write their own cases. Simply have each participant write up a short narrative of a real past situation that fits the topic that is being taught. Ask them to briefly write who was involved, when and where the event occurred, what was said or done, and their view of why it happened.

Then, if you have placed four participants at each table, pair the participants up and have them exchange this background information. After some additional preparation time, each participant will in turn be the individual in the situation they wrote about, and their partners will pretend to be them. The cost is time. It takes considerable time for the participants to write out their own cases and then prepare to practice them. But if it is critical that the participants "buy into" the skill practice session, extra time spent here could pay off well.

CHAPTER 7.
CLOSING

☑ 7. CLOSING

Four major tasks are normally addressed at the close of a program: 1) summarizing, 2) evaluating, 3) discussing the application of the program's ideas, and, 4) obtaining commitment from the participants to try what was learned.

Summarizing can help bring closure to a program by reviewing the key ideas and concepts that were discussed during the session. Simply using your program outline—or a prepared flip chart or transparency—will highlight the major areas covered during the program. At this time you can also ask for any additional questions or comments (given, of course, that you have time).

The close is also a good time to either evaluate the program, or explain your plans for evaluation that will occur later. Program evaluation can be conducted orally by breaking the group into sub-groups, and asking each group to elect a leader and anonymously record their comments on easel paper. You might ask questions such as:

> What did you like about today's program?
> What have you learned that is especially useful?
> What topic or topics do you wish we would have spent more time on?
> What topic or topics should we have spent less time on?
> What should we have covered in today's program that we didn't?
> How could the program have been improved for you?

Give the groups 8 to 10 minutes to complete their assignment, and then call time and ask the group leaders to report their group's work. When the reports are made, do not get defensive! Avoid, if possible (this can be difficult), attempting to explain why you did what you did. Do feel free to ask questions if you don't understand a comment, or if the comment is too general to be useful. But for the most part, simply sit quietly, take notes, and then sincerely thank the leaders for their reports.

A similar type of evaluation can be conducted by passing out evaluation sheets, and asking the participants to complete them—anonymously—and lay them upside down on the table before they leave. Many facilitators have learned the importance of collecting written evaluations before the participants leave in order to reduce retrieval problems later.

Conducting evaluations immediately at the close of a program has the advantage of the experience being fresh in the participants' minds. As a result, they can remember better—and provide more feedback on—what happened in the program.

However, there is an important disadvantage in conducting evaluations at the close of the training session rather than at a later time. Unfortunately, closing evaluations are notorious for overrating programs. This occurs because of special things that happen to groups toward the end of a program. The participants feel good. They may have worked hard, and have a deep sense of accomplishment. They have learned to know each other, worked together, and view you in a position of trust and authority—such feelings are often reflected in evaluations that are strongly biased in a positive direction.

Scheduling and conducting evaluations with the participants at a later time can be accomplished by mailing the written evaluation form to them. Or, interviews can be scheduled with each participant, and the evaluations conducted orally. Note, too, that combinations of the above strategies may be used.

Another key task to be completed at the close of a training program is determining how the participant plans to utilize what has been learned. This "application" question can often be combined with an oral evaluation, or even placed on the written evaluation form. Thus, you may ask:

What specific things have you learned today?
How can these things be applied in your job to help you be even more effective?

Another way of helping the participants make the classroom to job transition at the close of the workshop is the following:

A. Ask each participant to write down three things that he or she learned during the workshop.

B. Next, ask each person to write what they will DO differently as a result of each of the three things they learned.

C. Last, ask each participant in turn to publicly commit to one of the three items on his or her list. As you hear their responses, be as challenging as necessary to help the participants be specific about their future actions.

For example, suppose you have just finished a workshop on "Managing Time," and Betty reports, "I'm going to be better organized." You might respond by asking, "What do you plan to do to get better organized?" "Clean off my desk," Betty says. "Great," you respond. "When do you plan to have your desk completely organized?" "Well," Betty says, "I guess I'll have it finished in two weeks." "OK. that will make it around the 23rd of this month. Is that about right?" "Right!" Betty replies.

"All right," you ask, "who here sees Betty on a regular basis?" At this point, Tom states that he sees Betty on a regular basis. You then ask Tom if he would be willing to stop by Betty's work area sometime on the 23rd and take a look at her desk. If it looks good, he will give her some positive feedback. If it is still messy, he will ask when he can reinspect it.

Go around the room in this way, asking each participant what he or she plans to change back on the job. Set up pairs of people to follow up with each other if necessary. Some of the best sessions I have observed were those where this strategy was used to stimulate concrete results back on the job.

CHAPTER 8.
FOLLOWING UP

☑ 8. FOLLOWING UP

At the close of the training session, show a sign-up sheet and ask the participants to select a time and date for a follow-up meeting with you. Then, during the follow up meetings, ask each one what he or she has done to apply the things they learned in the session. Give positive reinforcement for the things they have tried, answer any questions they may still have, and make suggestions for additional application if appropriate.

The primary responsibility for training and developing the participants that attend your programs belongs to the manager of those participants. Our role as trainers is to help managers with this responsibility — not to replace them in it. The managers of the people who will be attending your training sessions must feel that any training you do is a part of their employee's ongoing plan of development. These managers need to know what will be taught to their people, what the participants should do with the knowledge they gain in the training program, and what you need from management to support the concepts that are taught.

Therefore, one of the best strategies for follow-up is to involve the participants' bosses. This is based on the philosophy that training will be most effective when the organizational climate supports the basic ideas taught. Therefore, before the training program begins, present the managers with an overview of the topics that will be covered, and ask for their support. This overview can, of course, be conducted after the session(s) with the employees. But if it is conducted prior to the sessions, it will help reduce participant comments like, "This is a great program, but you know who ought to be here? My boss!"

Generally, training the managers of the people who will be attending your training sessions follows this general format:

A. Give them a brief overview of the content of the training program. You can do this by presenting the key behaviors that will be taught, showing selected samples of any video tapes that will be used in the session, and clearly communicating the course objectives. The objectives will tell the managers exactly what their people should later be able to do on the job. The managers should be given a written copy of the program's objectives so that they do not have to depend on memory alone.

B. Tell the managers exactly what you expect them to do — both before and after the future training sessions. For example, you may wish to have them meet individually with their employees in order to prepare them for the session. Or, you may want the manager to conduct follow-up meetings with each of the participants after the training program is finished. You may also want the managers to give positive reinforcement to newly-learned behaviors that are exhibited by the employees. Whatever you wish the managers to do, let them in on the secret by telling them!

Unfortunately, managers sometimes find it easy to SAY they will follow up with their employees —but often don't! There are several partial solutions to this problem. First, you are going to have to follow up with the managers to ensure that they are doing what they agreed to do. Second, make sure that the executives of the organization are highly supportive of the training, and also have publicly expressed this support (especially to the managers). Finally, set up the performance appraisal system so that the managers are being rated on how well they follow up and support the training that their people receive.

One thing is certain: the more the managers are involved in the entire training process, the more support you will have from them. This means that they need to be a part of the original needs assessment, be consulted on the training content and design, and even play a role in the training itself if possible.

C. Finally, ask the managers for feedback and/or questions.

SUGGESTED READING

SUGGESTED READING

Bard, Ray, et al. *The Trainer's Professional Development Handbook*. San Francisco: Jossey-Bass, 1987.

Craig, Robert L. *Training and Development Handbook* (ASTD, 3rd Edition). New York: McGraw-Hill, 1987.

Custer, Gene E. *Planning, Packaging, and Presenting Training*. San Diego: University Associates, 1986.

Draves, William A. *How to Teach Adults*. Manhattan, Kansas: The Learning Resources Network, 1984.

Eitington, Julius E. *The Winning Trainer: Winning Ways to Involve People in Learning*. Houston: Gulf, 1984.

Margolis, Fredric H., and Bell, Chip R. *Instructing for Results* (Rev. ed.). San Diego: University Associates, 1986.

Mayo, Douglas G. and DuBois, Philip H. *The Complete Book of Training: Theory, Principles, and Techniques*. San Diego: University Associates, 1987.

Reddy, W. Brendan and Henderson, Clenard C. *Training Theory and Practice*. San Diego: University Associates, and Arlington: NTL Institute, 1987.

Renner, Peter Franz. *The Instructors' Survival Kit* (Rev. ed.). Vancouver, B.C., Canada: Training Associates Ltd., 1983.

Smith, Barry J., and Delahaye, Brain L. *How to Be an Effective Trainer*. New York: Wiley, 1987.

Tracey, William R. *Human Resources Management and Development Handbook*. New York: AMACOM, 1985.

Zemke, Ron, et al. *Designing and Delivering Cost-Effective Training and Measuring the Results*. Minneapolis: Lakewood Publications, 1981.

SELF-STUDY

INSTRUCTIONS FOR SELF-STUDY

1. If available, complete the Pre-test. Grade this test using the scoring key and note the number of questions you got right.

2. Play the videotape titled, "At Least There Were Refreshments." If this videotape is not available, read the script found on pages 79–83. Locate self-study page 78, and list all of the ways that the trainer could have been more effective. Then, check your list against the list found on pages 84–85.

3. Read the Equipment and Training Room Layout sections in the Participant's Manual (pgs. 1–20).

4. Read the balance of the Participant's Manual (pgs. 21–73),including the topics of Preparing, Opening, Asking, Advising, Assimilating, Applying, Closing, and Following Up.

5. Play the Positive Model videotape.

6. If available, complete the Post-test. Grade this test using the scoring key and note the number of questions you got right. Then, compare your Post-test score with your Pre-test score. These two tests are equivalent, so that any increase in your score should be due to your increased knowledge. Note that each question is keyed to a specific section of your Participant's Manual. If you find that a question was answered incorrectly, review that question's section in the Participant's Manual.

THIS PAGE FOR SELF-STUDY ONLY
NEGATIVE MODEL VIDEO ANALYSIS

Play the videotape, "At Least There Were Refreshments." As the tape is playing, list below all the ways that the trainer could have improved his training session. See how many of approximately 40 items you can identify, and then compare your list with the list on pages x and xi. If the videotape is not available, identify — and write below — as many of the 40 items as possible by reading the script that follows on pages v-ix.

1. _____

2. _____

3. _____

4. _____

5. _____

6. _____

7. _____

8. _____

9. _____

10. _____

11. _____

12. _____

13. _____

14. _____

15. _____

16. _____

17. _____

18. _____

19. _____

20. _____

21. _____

22. _____

23. _____

24. _____

25. _____

26. _____

27. _____

28. _____

29. _____

30. _____

31. _____

32. _____

33. _____

34. _____

35. _____

36. _____

37. _____

38. _____

39. _____

40. _____

FOR SELF-STUDY USE ONLY

"AT LEAST THERE WERE REFRESHMENTS"

VIDEO SCRIPT

Narrator: Training, one of the most rewarding jobs there is—when it is done well. It can also be a bad experience, for both the trainer and the participants, when it is done poorly. Let's look at a trainer as he conducts a workshop on "Performance Appraisal."

(It is a typical classroom: an overhead projector and a screen in the front of the room, empty tables and chairs arranged classroom style, blackboard with an eraser but no chalk, one flip chart already full, and coffee in the back of the room. Several of the participants are seated at the table, several more are back at the coffee urn, and a third group is standing talking to each other. There is a total of 12 participants.)

(At that moment the trainer, Bob, walks through the open door, leaving it open, carrying a large briefcase.)

Bob: Hi, everybody! (He walks up to the front of the room, drops his attache case on the table, and starts pulling things out of the case and putting them on the table.), Why don't you grab a seat, and let's get started? (Still pulling things out of his attache case.) I'm Bob Williams, and I am going to be your instructor for the day.

(The participants finish their conversations, and slowly begin to find places to sit.)

Bob: It's 8:30, so I guess we better get started. Let's see, who is here? I count (he does a quick head count) 12 of you; and I have 14 on my list. Let me call the roll to see who is missing. Bud?

(He calls each name in turn: Bud, Laura, Carol, Lydia, Yvonne, Linda, Connie, Lorrie, Kim, Mike, Ruth, Joe, Frances, and Sue. The participants respond with "Here," "Present," "Yo," etc. Lydia and Mike are not in the room. By the time Bob is finished calling the roll, all the participants are seated.)

Bob: Anybody know where Lydia and Mike are? (Short pause.) OK. Why don't we give them a few more minutes?

(Some participants start to talk to each other, and others look around. Bob continues to get the front table organized. He opens up a well-worn leader's guide, lays a couple of transparencies by the projector, and looks at one of the transparencies, noticing that it wasn't cleaned from the last time it was used. He pulls out a small cloth and cleans the old writing off the transparency. He checks the blackboard to see if there is an eraser and chalk. He finds the eraser, but there is no chalk. While the participants talk with each other—the noise level gradually rising—Bob leaves the room. He is gone for a minute, and returns holding a piece of chalk. He walks back to the front of the room, and at that moment Mike walks in. Bob, turning, sees Mike.)

79

Bob: You must be (looks at list) . . . Mike?

Mike: Right. (Mike looks around, finds an empty chair, and sits down.)

Bob: (Looks at wrist watch.) Let's wait another minute for Lydia.

            (Bob walks back to the coffee urn and gets a cup of coffee. He stirs in sugar and powdered cream, and then walks back to the front. Mike notices Bob's coffee, and goes back and gets himself a cup.)

Bob: (Looks at his watch again.) OK, I guess we'd better get started. (Some participants continue talking, while others begin to quiet down.) As you know, the topic for today is "Conducting Effective Performance Appraisals." (Bob walks to the easel, flips over the sheets that have already been written on, and discovers that the pad is full. He then walks over to the blackboard and writes "Performance Appraisal" on the board in cursive handwriting.) Mike, what is the reason you signed up for today's session?

Mike: My boss made me. (General laughter.)

Bob: I guess that's a good enough reason. (Bob picks up the first of his transparencies, places it on the projector, and turns on the light. He focuses the projector and moves the screen to the correct angle. The transparency's print is too small, obviously made with a typewriter.) OK, I'd like to spend some time this morning talking about why we need to conduct good appraisal interviews, and then the balance of the time talking about how we should do it. My guess is that most of you now conduct performance appraisals. Since we will be covering a lot of information today that you may need to use the next time you conduct a performance appraisal, you should take notes. (Several of the participants get out pens and note pads.)

            In addition, there will be a short quiz at the end of today's session, and the results —or, scores — will go back to your bosses. (More people get out note paper and pads, and pencils). OK, do you have any questions? (Pauses briefly.)

            (Looks back at overhead projector screen as he talks.) Let's take a look at the four factors that affect the quality of a performance appraisal. First are the environmental issues. Issues like: does your boss support you by giving you the time it takes to prepare and conduct quality interviews? (Turns and walks back to the overhead projector and, using his finger, points out the next item as he talks. Lydia walks into the room. Bob sees her but keeps on talking. Lydia looks around, sees an empty chair, and walks over to it and sits down.)

            The second factor is the paperwork system. Now our system is outstanding. We've got great performance appraisal forms that anybody can use. (Camera catches Bud looking at another participant with a look of disgust, and the second participant nods her head back and forth, lowering her face into her hands. It is obvious that Bob sees the non-verbals, but he chooses to ignore them.) And the personnel department has done a terrific job of setting up the system.

That leads us to the third factor, and that's you. Do you know how to really conduct an effective performance appraisal, and do you have the skills to do it?

And the last factor is the employee that is being appraised. What is his attitude toward the interview, and how much time is he given to prepare for it?

When an organization sees that their performance appraisal system is not working, the first thing they do to fix the problem is to change the form. Several years ago, some of you may recall that we had a pretty lousy form. (Bud raises his hand.) But, the one we... (sees Bud's hand is up, but ignores it for the moment)... have now is outstanding! Therefore, we will spend most of the day dealing with the interview itself. We'll discuss how to prepare for it, and then how to conduct it. (Bud's hand is still up.) In addition, we will also look at the interview from the employee's point of view. We'll take a look at how we can help him prepare for the interview , and what his responsibility will be in it. Yes... (looks down at his roster)... uh, Bill?

Bud: Bud.

Bob: Right. Bud. You have a question?

Bud: I have a great deal of difficulty using the new form.

Bob: I'm sure that by the end of the day you will see how it fits the interview. Why don't you hold any questions on the form until we finish up today's session, and if we have time at the end, let's see if your questions aren't answered. Now, as I was saying... (Camera fades to black and comes up on Bob. A new transparency is on the projector.)

Bob: OK, I've finished the first two steps in conducting a peformance appraisal, and it's 10:30. Let's take a 15-minute break and start in again at 10:45. (Bob turns off the projector. The rest of the group begins to stand, some move toward the coffee urn, and others head for the door. Bob walks out of the room without saying anything more. Camera fades to black.)

(The scene opens with the participants seated. They are talking to each other. Bob walks in. He looks at his watch.)

Bob: Sorry I'm a few minutes late. OK, where were we? (Turns on the projector.) Right. Now step three is where we discuss with the employee any concerns we have with his performance that he has not already brought up for discussion.

Now this step is a mini-counseling model that you can use year 'round. Note that in Step A we describe in very specific terms exactly what the employee has done that he shouldn't have done—or should have done, but didn't. Then, in Step B, we tell the employee what we expect. Next, in Step C, we ask the employee for the cause of the situation. And in Step D, we ask the employee for a solution. But since the supervisor already knows what the employee needs to do, why not just tell him?

Carol: But since the supervisor already knows what the employee needs to do, why not just tell him?

Bob: (He glances at his watch. As he begins to reply to this question, Bob is looking at Carol.) The answer to that is obvious. If we tell the employee what to do, then the solution is "our" solution, not the employee's. (Carol shows no apparent response. Bob then looks at the other people in the group as he finishes his answer.)

The employee is not invested in the solution—since it is ours—and has little motivation to make the solution work. In addition, even though we think our solution is always best, it might not be. The employee might surprise us and come up with a better solution than ours. It is the same reason that we ask the employee, in Step C, for the cause of the problem. By asking the employee to identify the cause, we increase his awareness of the problem. And he might, in fact, reveal a real cause of the problem that we hadn't seen.

Connie: (Interrupting.) But isn't there a danger that the employee will suggest a solution that is totally impractical?

Bob: (As Bob begins to answer Connie's question, Connie nods her head in agreement as he talks. As he continues to talk, he looks only at her, ignoring the rest of group.) Not really. I'll tell you what. Let's take just a minute and look at a terrific model of decision making and problem solving developed by Norman R.F. Maier.

(Bob turns to the front table, picks up a red magic marker, and walks over to the easel. As he reaches the easel, he suddenly remembers that it has no clean sheets. He walks back toward the table, tosses the marker back on the table, moves the projector screen over, turns off the projector light, looks around for the chalk, finds it, and begins to write on the board.)

Bob's drawing

Employee's solutions				Supervisor's solutions
Z	Not OK		OK	P

Maier said, let this line (draws a horizontal line) represent a continuum of ideas or solutions, and let this end (writes a "P" at the right end of the horizontal line) represent all those ideas that are perfect. Then, let the other end represent all those ideas that have zero value (writes a "Z" at the left hand end of the line). In other words, the ideas at this end are utterly worthless.

Now Maier said that we seldom see ideas or solutions at either end of this line. In fact, almost all ideas, even the employees', lie somewhere on the line, between the two end points. Now let this vertical line (draws a vertical line upward, starting at the center point of the horizontal line) represent a line that separates workable solutions from those that are not workable. All workable solutions fall somewhere to the right of this line, and the unworkable ones on the left. Now let's say that you are the supervisor in this situation. Automatically, on which side of the line does your idea fall?

(Bob does not wait for an answer—it is a rhetorical question.) Right, the right side; and we probably see it as perfect. Now, if this is the first time the employee has been asked for his solution to this specific problem, which side of this line will his solution probably lie on? You bet! The left side. Maybe not totally worthless, but close.

So then, Maier says we play the "Yes, but..." game. We say, "Yes, but let me tell you how wrong you are..."—and proceed to save the day by offering our solution. Maier said don't do it! Try to get the employee's solution. If it is not a workable solution at first glance, ask questions, offer suggestions, and see if both of you can move that idea to the other side of the OK/Not OK line. If the idea, in the final analysis, is not workable, the employee will likely see that. At that point, you can ask the employee for another solution. Or if necessary, offer your own.

(Bob glances at his watch.) Wow, look at the time. It looks like we're going to run a little over today in order to get finished.

OK, back to the model. Let's look at the next step, Step #4. Now in this step....

(Camera fades to black and comes up on the narrator.)

Narrator: Well, the workshop participants are going to have the pleasure of working past the announced quitting time. I wonder how those who have families waiting, or are in car pool arrangements, are feeling about that?

Granted, what you have just seen is an extreme example—of over 40 things—of what not to do in a workshop. But it's not really that extreme. I'll bet many of you have experienced most, if not all, of the things that this trainer did—at one time or another. And it's not an "accident" when poor training occurs. It happens because poorly trained people are given opportunities to subject others to their lack of training.

You see, good training doesn't just happen. It is planned, and then conducted, by trainers who have a total understanding of the dynamics of facilitating groups.

As trainers, we have a special responsibility—the responsibility to be the very best that we can be in order that the training we do will create positive results for our trainees and for our organizations.

As John Kennedy once said, "It is time for a new generation of leadership to cope with new problems and new opportunities. For there is a new world to be won."

TRAINER'S PROBLEMS

In order to help you evaluate your list of the trainer's problems, compare it with the following.

1. Arrived late.

2. Room was set up in "classroom" style.

3. Didn't greet individual participants.

4. Had not prepared the room in advance.

5. Projector screen was in the wrong location.

6. The transparencies were not cleaned prior to the session.

7. Didn't have his supplies lined up in advance (chalk).

8. Didn't have new, clean easel pad.

9. Didn't start on time (waited for late arrivals).

10. Wrote on the blackboard in cursive rather than block print (cursive is more difficult to read from the back of the room).

11. Singled out Mike for his first question (better to ask the group as a whole rather than single out one individual).

12. Didn't elicit the group's expectations or needs.

13. Didn't use learning objectives.

14. Didn't set up the overhead projector in advance.

15. Transparency print was too small.

16. Didn't know who in the group actually conducted performance appraisals.

17. No handouts.

18. Referenced a quiz with the results to be sent to participants' bosses.

19. Asked a "closed" question ("Do you have any questions?") rather than an "open" question ("What questions do you have?").

20. Did not give the participants time to respond to his question.

21. Initially looked at the projector screen rather than at the participants as he talked.

22. Made such a strong point about how great the present performance appraisal system was that he was not likely to discover the participants' concerns.

23. Used finger rather than a pointer (pencil or pen) to indicate items on the transparency.

24. Didn't acknowledge Lydia's presence when she entered the room.

25. Ignored participants' non-verbal signals about the performance appraisal form and system.

26. Should have checked with the participants whether or not the performance appraisal system and form were working for them.

27. Used only masculine pronouns throughout.

28. Training format was limited to lecture.

29. Participants felt they had to raise their hands to be recognized.

30. Initially ignored a participant's raised hand.

31. No identification name tags on the tables.

32. Didn't remember the participant's name.

33. Didn't find out what difficulty a participant was having with the form.

34. Delayed answering the participant's question until the end of the program.

35. Late coming back from break.

36. Looked at watch.

37. Should have relayed Carol's question back to the group rather than answering it himself.

38. Put Carol down by saying, "The answer to that is obvious."

39. Did not check out with Carol whether or not he had answered her question.

40. Could have referred Connie's question back to the group.

41. Got sidetracked by the Maier discussion.

42. Got trapped by the "head nodder," and did not include the rest of the group in the Maier discussion.

43. Didn't manage his time well.

44. Risked participants becoming hostile due to staying after quitting time.